Word da

By Bryan Griffin & Ro

An imaginative poetic journey from horror to humour and all in between

Word Dancing by Bryan Griffin & Rowland Crowland

© Bryan Sydney Griffin. Rowland Crowland

Year of Publication 2021

To Peter

Best Wishes

Bryan

Dedication

To our wives Sue and Ann without whose support and patience we would never have performed or put pen to paper

Preface

We both moved to Morecambe around the same time and as poets we met whilst performing at a well-known Lancaster Spoken Word venue. We quickly became firm friends and performed at various venues and on Radio together.

Although our styles and delivery were different, audiences seemed to enjoy how we complemented each other's performance. It seemed a natural progression to collaborate and produce this book.

Introduction

Bryan Griffin an award-winning performing poet. His poetry has been published in anthologies and magazines both in the UK and internationally this is his third book. As well as producing and hosting cultural and talk shows for Northwest Lancashire's Beyond Radio he has performed and been interviewed on various TV programmes, BBC Radio, commercial radio stations. After moving to Morecambe he created with the Mayor's office an Annual Lancaster Junior Poet Laureate competition and provides free workshops for Schools. He is still regularly featured in events including the Morecambe Fringe and has been guest performer twice at the Edinburgh Fringe. Bryan continues to provide workshops and works with and performs for many charitable and community causes.

Rowland Crowland is an author and performing poet from Manchester who now lives in Morecambe. Known as the Goblin Poet, he performs at pubs, clubs, theatres and festivals across the Northwest. He is well known for his expressive delivery which is invariably unusual but always captivating, as can be seen on his YouTube channel. His poetry is earthy and uncompromising and often conveys tragicomedy at its most unnerving. Rowland is regularly featured on local radio and often performs live with Bryan. This is his second book.

Bryan Griffin: Dances on the Darkside
Horror/Black Humour

The welcome stranger

The timber wolf's howling sounded as if it were some lonely
tune
But he was just having his nightly debate with the waxing
moon.
It stopped suddenly alert, still, sensing some danger
approaching.
Suddenly it loped away, fearful of whatever was
encroaching.
Its fear, a feral growl lingered as a fading echo amongst tall
trees.
The wood stirred, birds flew, game fled for they too felt
danger.
The grassy path and nearby leaves withered, heralding the
stranger.
The woodcutter's cabin windows emitted a warm oil lamp
glow
 Log fire smoke escaped the chimney, spiralled upward lazy
and slow,
The door opened; a shaft of light stabbed out into the dark
gloom.
The old man's weak rheumy eyes expectantly peered into
the night.
Smiling, his arms beckoning the stranger welcome, he felt
no fright.

"I've been expecting you friend, a chairs ready by the fire, come in."
The stranger entered, giving the old man some semblance of a grin,
"Sit down my friend" the woodcutter said "have some hot rum and tea."
Proffering his tobacco leaf; they both lit pipes happily content,
"A game of chess?" the old man asked, the stranger nodded assent.
After studying the chess board awhile, the stranger moved his pawn.
The old man moved his, in companiable silence they played till dawn.
Slowly standing up the grim stranger readied himself to take his leave
The old man spoke; "I hoped perhaps this time you had come for me,
My wife and child lie buried seasons since, I long to join my family.
I know the dread plague has offered many souls for you to reap
You're weary from your toil, but my ancient bones yearn to sleep.
Fare thee well, perhaps next time my friend" he sadly said to the stranger.
"Perhaps," the visitor thought continuing again his journey alone.
The old man smiled "In god's good time," re-entering his home.

Striding on the visitor knew he must collect the old man in the end.

He'd been on the list some time but even death appreciated a friend,

Still, he could at least delay until the plague had taken its mounting due.

Down in the valley

Down, down in the valley, a primordial spirit sleeps, here no Chapel bells ring or sing songbird cheeps, for over its meadows and streams evil doth creep.

Down, down in the valley, lives something so fell, its malign spirit casts some terrible demonic spell subordinating all with its malevolent compel.

Deep, deep in the vale within an aged copse evil does dwell entrancing young maidens to its dell where amidst bent twisting trees they enter hell.

Deep, deep is a hunger only a life can feed, for a sacrifice each season must answer the soils need, with each harvest renewal a human heart must bleed.

Down, down in the dale the passage toll is dear for deep, deep in the valley visitors pay the price of fear for within this vale a dark malignancy rules all here.

Freight train

Clickityclack, clickityclickityclack, clickityclack.
Death hurls heedless down the railway track,
Onward it hurtles forth in its headlong attack
As if lit by perditions fires it hisses and steams,
Its noisome engine hiding the terrible screams.

Clickityclack, clickityclickityclack, clickityclack.
As the girl's body suffers its bloody mutilated fate
The carriage grabs her soul to add to its freight.
Leaving the remains Death continues its ride,
Steaming onward in pursuit of the next suicide.

Clickityclack, clickityclickityclack, clickityclack,
Death hurls heedless down the railway line,
All aboard, next stop hell and deaths on time.

I Monster

I saw in the dark rippling waters my own reflection and dropped her raggedy doll shocked by my imperfection.

Lost in my anguish I held the little girl so very, very tight as I tried to protect her innocence from the hideous sight.

I held her close, so close I felt my heart would burst. She went limp so limp then I knew I Monster was cursed.

For Monster or Innocent, we must follow the Fates call, thus, bidden by their whims, they make victims of us all.

The Silent Farewell

The old man sits in his rocking chair staring out from the front porch upon the busy vista of a hot dusty street. Wearing his Confederate jacket, his one hand resting upon a small table grasping an iced glass of Julip minty sweet. Buzzing flies sip salty beads of sweat from a face shaded by a cavalry hat and the rim of the sugary sweet glass. Passers-by greet the familiar figure of the colonel, others wave from their horse drawn buggies as they pass. The gardens sweet oleander perfume lingers and lies heavy in the warm sultry air almost masking a sicklier sweet smell.The Grandfather Clock was silent, it usually permeated the porch with its loud tick-tock and hourly chiming bell. A large frog jumps upon the table voicing a loud quizzical Nideep at the strangely still figure before leaping away. The Colonel unmoved with unseeing eyes stared silently out at the gathering dusk heralding the dying of the day.

Carpe Diem

Opportunity Came knocking on his door unfortunately Death had called three hours before.

The House on the Hill

The House on the hill, a place where glory departed so long ago,
Dust covers drape the furniture and pictures of long forgotten pride.
The once hurly burl of life diminished to a faint whispered echo
Of aging doors creaking stirred by the musty air that drafts provide.

The atmosphere heavy, pensive, musty with the stillness of a Tomb.
Broken by a mournful clock as it strikes the chimes of midnight.
Occasional car headlight's flash brief shafts of light pierce the gloom Making the rats and mice run madly hither thither in startled fright.

Dust from the plaster gently falls as if weeping from dark shame.
What horrors or catastrophes occurred making this place so lone?
Moonlights luminosity eerily reflects the House of Ushers name.
What caused such lonely desolation, why desert this manorial home.

A night at the museum

Something wrong stirred amidst relics and old bones, it seemed to pervade all, as if something palpable and menacing was seeping through every wall.

The boiler was working, thermostats set to normal yet the air was cold, the lights died suddenly the night guard shuddered as a chill took hold.

Frosty condensation appeared upon a glass display casement but the guard did not notice as he made his way to the fuse box in the basement.

Torchlight dancing, the way ahead abruptly dimmed as he opened the basement door, in the darkness he shook the sputtering torch preparing to descend to its floor.

Stopping he heard coming from the basement below a scrabbling sound, panicked rats ran blindly past as from a sinking ship in fear of being drowned.

Like a tidal wave they flowed up the steps squealing in alarm as they raced by. The guard froze transfixed in horror until their terrible squealing was a distant cry.

Hands shaking, wiping his cold brow, he turned peering down the corridor now in darkness. It seemed menacingly evil, he thought perhaps it was just stress.

Frightened he peered into the dark, a sound, he heard it again, was it something dragging? A sweet pervading sickly stench of death so pungent set him gagging.

The torch flickered showing a slow ambling, limping, horror bandages loosely hanging, seeing its menacing intent to attack, he stepped back heart fiercely banging.

The shocked curator stood staring at the body on the basements bloodstained floor. 'As I understand it, 'the policemen said 'He fell as he came through the door.'

 'I don't know why George was carrying a dirty smelly bandage in his hand, I must go Officer the new display of the Mummy Pa'Hotep is still to be planned.'

Vampiric

My soul was taken with a Judas kiss. Its terrible curse brought me to this, forever to walk in the shadow of night hungrily gifting a necrophiliac bite.

Never again to gaze at the dawning of day, from its burning kiss I must hideaway to escape into the safety of my grave. Only in dark can I seek the blood I crave

I am become life's corrupt counterfeit, there is no warmth, no love in it. Just endless hunger, an endless need to bite into flesh and bloodily feed.

For now, I'm a hunter predatorily cruel, A tainted creature, a demonic tool my soul was stolen with a Judas kiss, its terrible curse brought me to this.

Griffin Noir

The darkened streets and alleyways seem pensive in shadowy dark, as the last tip tap of footsteps echo distantly down the shop strewn winding way called main street.

All is hushed as the echo dies leaving a gentle hiss of drizzle falling haphazard on paved slabs, then to a deeper pitter pat as the misty rain changes to a raindrop beat.

A nerve jangling, hair raising, curdling screech of an angry cat, feral and primitive rips forth, raw and harsh, as with all screams it quickly dies to merge into the gentle rain's song.

A bright red cigarette glow dies and glows again in a distant doorway almost hidden by the blur of rain, as if in warning it's red ember flickers as it is inhaled deep and strong.

A dustbin lid jangled, disturbed by a mistral gust of breeze whispering in swirling whirls sending the raindrops skitter scat as it helter-skeltered on its haphazard way.

A solid wall of penetrating, sapping cold rises like a spectre from the grave, exposed flesh shivers, goose bumps tingle as its freezing bite holds all in its sway.

From the doorway expelled breath turns to hoary mist as it hits the cold air and hovers in shock. A cigarette like a firefly soars from a darkened doorway to crash down into the gutter.

Suddenly on the opposite side a light harshly glares from a window. A shuffle of feet, a shadow emerges as a foot swiftly extinguishes the cigarette's dying sputter.

Curtains swiftly drawn hide the bright light, a shadowy figure with fleet stealth flows quietly across the road unheard, unseen, even by a slow passing police car.

The headlights catching the rain like moths trapped in an ethereal glow, steamed windows glisten and sparkle as rivulets flow its blue light flashing like some distant star.

As the car travels slowly to be lost in the night's gloom a blanket of silence fell, disturbed briefly by glass breaking, a tinkling sing song then eerie stillness as in a dream.

Nothing stirred. Silent as the grave the darkened shadows nervously seemed awaiting some looming calamity, then, a loud bang engulfed by a long lingering scream.

A door slammed as the darkened streets and alleyways awoke to the last of the hollow tip tap of footsteps distantly echoing down the shop strewn winding way called main street.

Love ?

Each day I stand cold and reluctant at her grave,
for even in death, I am forever her unwilling slave.
Upon her beauteous splendour now feasts the worm, the
sheer ghastly horror of it makes my stomach turn.
Her stern beauty and steely in- dominate will is a
maddening compulsion drawing me to her still.

Her love was total contemptuous enslavement; I the added
spice for her foul appetite, a mere condiment
She bent me totally to her sordid lustful depravity,
perverting my whole essence, the very soul of me
Even now she is gone I find no comfort in sleeping, in both
life and death I am hers alone, forever in her keeping

For one night she came back to me in a vile dream
feverishly I awoke with terror and in horror I did scream
For my body was in a lover's tryst of rotting flesh wrapped
in her lustful skeletal embrace I was trapped.
So now when hesitantly I surrender to dread sleep, from
her grave licentiously to my bed she doth creep.

Each day I stand cold and reluctant at her grave,
for even in death, I am forever her unwilling slave.

Diner

Light from the diner window illuminates the darkened street, invading the gloom and glistening upon the paved concrete.

Inside refugees from the cold linger over coffee and bagels, as cigarette smoke dances blue swirls amongst cooling smells.

Outside wintery rain falls gently, whispering a pitter-patter beat, its misty cascade making streetlamps dimly radiate their defeat.

The patron's bodies shared the warmth but nothing more, for their thoughts seemed fixed upon some distant shore.

As the waitress buzzed and busily flitted with false Bonomi, taking their orders with world-weary attempts to be friendly.

As she served them coffee or plates of anything with chips, her fixed smile reflecting the jaded hope of generous tips.

As people slowly leave their homes in the growing light of day cars and buses speedily pass the diner on their busy way.

The diner's bell heralds its jingling notes of coming and going, as tables fill the footsore waitress sighs as if somehow knowing

That the chiming bell was tolling yet another cold wintery day, as crowds of alone merge to wander along the madden way.

Tears of love or hate for the White Rose?

Death seemed to become her, a stilled beauty so pale, the clear blue eyes fixed upon some distant vale.

Those generous, sensuous lips tinged blue from ruby red, her sultry voice hypnotic so dulcet now muted.

Forever silenced, her honeyed lies no longer reign, her lithe body now a white mannequin of porcelain.

Like some plucked rose whose white blossoms still delight with a temporary splendour suspending deaths blight.

Not even my sorrowful watering of gentle tears as they fall will gainsay the forlorn effect of eventual corruptive pall.

Her exquisite beauty will fade into withering final decay, slowly to be consumed in the unrelenting cold, cold clay.

The last rose petal

Laden by tears of dew the last rose petal fell in graceful silence to the bitter ground.
A delicate perfection slowly succumbing to corruption, as all things must

Forgotten in the crowd

He lay wrapped in a pool of red like some discarded toy, dead.

I still ponder the reason why he was so determined to die.

To slowly bleed out the gift of life by slicing his wrists with a knife.

What sorrow was so complete that it caused such utter self-defeat?

He always seemed to be around discreetly merged in the background.

I did not know him all that well more an acquaintance truth to tell.

I might say hello, briefly chat, admittedly little more than that.

I cannot give a viable reason why I was so troubled that he should die.

With feelings of consternation, I attended the service of his cremation.

On entering the chapel to my despair, I found no other mourners there.

How lonely it must be for one to be known by many but missed by none

And in that moment, I comprehended that here was a man unfriended.

Finally, travelling my way home I realised that now I too was alone.

For although known to many was there truly a friend amongst any

And will the hurly burl of the crowd just be the wrapping of my shroud.

A World of Black and White

Fierce irritation,
Clacking angry demands,
Of single-minded bigotry.

Wanting more,
Flapping out spite,
In territorial want.

Never satisfied,
Pecking out Domain,
Belligerent in Greed.

Bad Neighbours,
To close for comfort,
In mannered humanity.

The world is full of Magpies.

Rowland Crowland: Dances on the Darkside
Horror/Black Humour

This is not me!

This is not me!
This is schizophrenia!
This is not me!
This is amnesia!
This is not me!
This is leukopenia!
This is not me!
This is dyskinesia!
I'm not what you see!
A mad man with a limp!
I'm not what you see!
Two wild staring eyes!
I'm not what you see!
A sad man picking dimps!
I'm not what you see!
A man who talks to the skies!
This is me!
A man disbelieved!
This is me!
A man disempowered!
And this is me!
A sentient being!
The jewel in the heart of a lotus flower!

The Wind hasn't got a Home

The wind can kick up a fuss,
It can stop the thrushes singing
In their homes in the bushes and hedgerows,
It can shake the tree top jackdaws,
And leave them all alarmed,
For the wind hasn't got a home.

The wind can throw up a storm,
It can rattle all the rooftops,
It can make your heart stop,
It leads leaves up the garden path,
And whistles of forthcoming doom,
For the wind hasn't got a home.

It pretends to be your friend,
The gentle penetrating wind,
It softly brushes your cheek,
And ruffles your clothes,
It brings honeysuckle to your nose,
And lifts you up,
Like crows,
Held, hovering,
Ragged, as it blows,
Then it goes,
And lets you down,
It blows your blanket,
On the ground,

As you picnic
On boiled eggs and wine,
A summer breeze can make you feel fine,
And chilled,
Reclined,
But all the time,
It wants to fill your sails,
And lead you into
Unrelenting gales,
And laugh around your head,
And blow your picnic to the birds instead,
And leave you all undone,
For the wind hasn't got a home.

If you're small,
The wind will steal your beach ball
If you're old,
It'll blow you so hollow cold,
You'll have to hold onto someone
Just to get along
The wind doesn't care about right or wrong,
It doesn't care
If all your birds have flown,
For the wind hasn't got a home.

If you stand on a high mountain top,
The wind will threaten you with the drop!
Let it do its worst,
Let it curse you,
Let it rant and rave,

And pick you up and shake you,
And dash you down and try to break you,
And put you in your grave.
Just yield and you'll be safe,
And forgive its cries and moans,
For even in this lofty place,
The wind is not at home.

Coronation Park

Coronation Park is a wonderful thing,
Where the poor working class can do anything
Leisurely in a municipal setting
And reap the rewards that fresh air brings,

Like increased production for their overlings
When they already live like kings...
And wouldn't condescend to visit such things....
Not even in the Summer....
Not even in the Spring!

Coronation Park,
Coronation Park,
They named it after the King,
Coronation Park,
Coronation Park,
And He hadn't done anything!

There are gravel paths where couples can walk,
And hold each other's hands

There are benches where you can sit and talk,
There's a stand, where bands play, called a bandstand.
There's a bit where you can play football,
And a slope for roly-poly,
For the kids there's swings,
Oh, the joy it brings,
And it's free to the poor and the lowly!

Coronation Park,
Coronation Park,
They named it after the King,
Coronation Park,
Coronation Park,
But He never did anything!

Let's all go to Coronation Park,
Let's all go on the swings,
Let's all take a picnic there,
There are so many brilliant things,
You can sit on the grass
And watch the trains go past,
You can run about and let off steam,
You can pretend to be
Like someone else,
Like in a beautiful dream!

There's a place you can sit if you go after dark,
And watch the twinkling lights of the town,
I think the King should go and sit there,
To watch everyone settling down
To a night of cold,

And nursing the old,
And trying to make fire from nowt,
And making ends meet,
And having nothing to eat,
And no money left over for snout!
He could watch mothers cry,
When their babies die,
Or polio leaves its mark,
Yes, I'm sure the King could see everything
From Coronation Park!

Coronation Park,
Coronation Park,
They named it after the King,
Coronation Park,
Coronation Park,
Would He ever do anything?

Dopium

We're living in one room,
Like Birds,
There's no room,
The words
We use
Are not human,
I'm assuming
Others don't brood
In this day and age,
Smothered, caged,

Twiddling our thumbs,
Sat around with other bums,
Waiting for some punk
To bring home the breadcrumbs,
There's no air,
Everywhere's
Thick smoke,
Yellow fug,
Opium's no joke,
It's smug,
It's not a fun drug!
It mucks you up,
It puts you down,
In a drugged-up dug out
For shutdown clowns,
The black death,
Breath's dense and brown
And sick as butter,
No wonder the shutters
Are all on a come down
The day this circus
Comes to this ghost town!
Look around!
Yeh! Look all around
The dark bunk corners of our shanty town,
At the yellow eyes
Of nervous breakdowns,
Of broken nerves,
A room full of birds
With heads bowed down,

Dumb as worms
Buried under ground,
The smoke wreaths surround
Like burial shrouds,
All humanity's
Disavowed,
As someone mouths
With sunken gums,
We're not De Quincy
Or Jean Cocteau,
Just you and me
With nowhere to go!
Once you step
Through that big black zero
The smoke blows home
"Where's the dream-gun,"
"Where's mi dream gone?"
Gone!
It's gone my friend,
Everything's gone!
There's just this room,
Yeh, this is the one,
The waiting room
Where the Reaper comes,
He'll bring you some gum,
You worthless bum!
So, wait your turn,
There's nowhere to run,
Just wait and burn

Your big black "O"
With its clown of smoke,
Your Chinese tobacco
Kaleidoscope
Of fractal dreams,
And whacked-out streams,
All of it fleeting,
What's it all meaning?
Nothing great,
It's far too late
To dream of reality,
In this state
There is no sanity
Or no insanity,
It's not humanity,
I tell you mate,

And we just follow
Like soot-black birds
With broken necks,
Barely living
In a crow-dead nest
Whence the birds have flown,
And the smoke has blown
The hope away
From Dopium.

Eggshells

I'm walking on eggshells,
Being careful how I step!
Now I'm on quicksand,
And slow but certain death.
Just how long can I hold my breath?
Is there any point to life?
Is there any hope left?
Life should be a safe trail,
Where the potential's limitless,
But mine's become a risky path,
Through the mines
Of mental illness.

I am no one

The sound of people having
Fun, and I am nowhere,
I am no one.

Ghost Realm

Whose are those feet
Twitching on the street?
Whose are those trousers and shirt?
That tie?
Those tattooed hands
Are not mine!
Whose are those
Bits of splintered teeth?
Beneath the street lights shine?
They're not mine
For I'm in the Ghost Realm…
Hit by a car,
Struck by lightning,
Punched on the jaw,
And things are not the same anymore.
It's dark,
And it's beginning to rain,
There's no crowd gathering
In the street lamp's glare
Because nobody knows,
Will anybody care?
I'm alone,
Will I be cold?
Will I be sad?
When someone does hold me,
And they gather round,
And get me to hospital,
And jump on my bones,
Will they say something profound?

Will somebody weep,
As they lower me
Into the ground?
And will there be nice words....
These tattooed hands, like birds,
Are not mine,
For I'm in the Ghost Realm,
For a time!

The Boy at the Window

There's a boy looking out through the window,
He's watching the children play,
He's not very well,
So, he has to stay in,
For the moment, his mum and dad say.

There's a boy looking out through the window,
He's watching the people go past,
Some going to work,
Some going to church,
And some to the shops near the grass.

There's a boy looking out through the window,
He's watching the cars on the road,
Some of them fast,
They're just flying past,
And there's lorries with big heavy loads.

There's a boy looking out through the window,
He's watching the seasons change,
The spring's all green,
All summer there's trees,
Then the Autumn blows leaves all away.

The window cleaner comes to the window,
He makes the boy laugh with his face,
With his mop and his scrim,
He cleans everything,
Then he knocks at the door for his pay.

There's a boy looking out through the window,
He watches as folk come and go,
He stands like a brave,
And smiles as he waves,
But it's more like goodbye than hello.

Now the curtains are closed at the window,
The winter has turned the sky grey,
The windows are clean,
But no one's to be seen,
There's no boy at the window today.

Ghost

Christine?
Christine? Where are you?
I saw you on the Cheetham Hill Road,
Looking like you were going somewhere,
Your eyes like black coals,
Are you a ghost now?
I opened my arms to you,
But you walked through me
Like you had somewhere to go,
Stay with me a moment,
But no!
You were gone,
I know,
To the ghost market
For a shopping trolley full of lager,
With your eyes like black marbles.
But I'll stay in case you come back this way,
I'll go stand,
Beyond time,
Beyond space,
At that place,
At the corner of Waterloo Road,
And I'll wait,
No matter how late,
And I'll hold
And I'll take you home,
With your eyes like black stones.

Just Another Morning

Something has startled the crows,
Those starlings might know something!
The jackdaws singing?
No!
Jackdaws don't sing!
They're signalling!
The shadow of a peregrine,
Quick, wings, screams,
Silences the green trees.
Here comes the stealer of breath,
In the golden dawn,
Strike!
The back of the neck
Breaks! Black, blood feathers,
Eyes white,
Beak cleft,
Fledglings left without breakfast,
The happy nest bereft,
In the warmth of the sun,
A mother's warning forgone,
And another morning has begun.

Like Rain

The trees had lost their lovely leaves,
And black clouds filled the sky,
The day I watched the one I love,
Wither away and die,
Everything returns to earth,
And everyone's the same,
So why have I stopped living,
And my tears still fall like rain?
Since the non-beginning,
Things have happened so,
Beings appear and walk the earth,
Until it's time for them to go,
And then they rot and feed the earth,
Then in the flowers grow,
And in the food we eat, they're there,
They're living in the trees and so,
Their beauty's all around us,
And they're with us every day,
So why do we stop living,
And our tears they fall like rain?

Mum

It's exciting, isn't it mum,
Waiting for Monday
For the bin men to come,
I can feel it,
When the lorry's on
Our street,
And everyone's on their feet,
It's like we're under attack,
They lift the bins up on their backs,
And dump 'em in the back of the truck,
It's just brilliant isn't it mum!

Tuesday's good, isn't it mum,
Waiting for the pop man to come,
The pop man doesn't really make a noise,
He's just there,
And if you miss him, it's not fair,
You've got to go a whole week without pop,
Unless you buy a bottle from the shop,
But it doesn't taste the same,
Does it mum.
Dandelion and Burdock, Sarsaparilla,
Proper lemonade in yellow bottles,
What'll we do if we miss him mum?
The pop man!
I listen out for him,
Don't I mum!

Wednesday's great isn't it mum,
Waiting for the coal man to come,
He's black as pitch isn't he mum,
And you've got to stay in when he comes!
What I like best,
Is his black leather studied vest,
That lets him carry the coal bags,
On his shoulder,
They're big as boulders aren't they mum.
When he chucks it in our bunker,
Everyone has to run for cover,
There's black smoke everywhere,
It gets everywhere doesn't it mum!

Friday's good isn't it mum,
Waiting for the rag and bone man to come,
And he shouts "rag and bone!"
Or something like that,
Miles before you see him! It's brilliant that!
And his horse clops up the street,
With blinkers on his eyes,
And if you give him old rags,
You get a donkey stone on Fridays,
Where does he get his donkey stones from mum?
The best bit, isn't it mum,
Is when the horse opens his bum,
And plop drops out,
And you can shovel it up,
For the garden mum!

But I used to love Saturday best mum,
Waiting for my dad to come,
I used to feel great,
When I saw him at the gate,
And he'd come in,
And I'd sit with him,
And he'd always buy me something,
Like a toy, or a ball,
And we'd play kick against the wall,
It all seems a long time ago,
He doesn't seem to come anymore,
Does he mum?

No Ego

You took everything I had,
To satisfy your greedy mind,
It's only now I understand
That nothing was ever really mine.
Except my ego,
My only real possession,
And when she goes,
Well, the mess I'm in,
Will go too,
And then I'll know,
How you,
Could pounce like a cat
And throw a friend at the ceiling,

Rag a brother in your dog's teeth,
With no feeling for his feelings,
Steal a lover,
Like a fox,
Back to your lair,
All the time grinning,
Because it's all about winning,
And always, ever has been
From the beginning,
Of time,
What's mine,
Is yours,
For the taking,
And even though my heart is breaking,
I know that
My emotions
Are fake things,
And someday I'll let them go,
And then, only then,
When there are no demons,
Will there be no ego.

Not Their Turn

When Bobby jumped off that building,
My heart dropped with him,
And smacked like jam on the tarmac.
Someone screamed,
He looked up at me apologetically,
His femurs where his shoulders should be,
He'd never get any older and
And he'd never go any further and
I wish that he'd been murdered,
Or he'd died of cancer
Because there's never any answer,
Or any understanding
When someone feels abandoned,
And dives off a verandah.
Or cuts themselves with a lager can ring pull,
Or hacks with a shard of broken pot,
Or fashions a rope from a nylon sock,
The knot,
Tight,
The size of a peanut,
Impossible to cut,
Or get your fingers in.
All these young people then,
Hurt or maimed or dead,
How can I ever rest
When instead
Of peace in my heart,
There's that dread
Sound as a head

Hits the ground,
Or a hack saw blade hacks an open wound,
The unexpected sizzle
Of skin under a cig burn,
All the sounds of young people,
Leaving,
Before it's their turn.

One More Day

Hey look!
The sun's coming up,
Come on, let's get up,
What do you say?
It's going to be beautiful out there,
Let's get up early today.
We'll go down the shops,
And see what's going on,
We'll have some breakfast,
Some eggs and bacon,
And we'll just watch
The world go by.
You can look in Primark ,
And New Look,
And I'll just buy a paper and sit in the sun,
And then I'll meet you for a coffee later on,
And we'll have a laugh, eh!
A skinny cappuccino
And a caramel latte.

We'll walk home,
It'll be good you'll see,
We'll get a bottle of white wine,
And some kippers for tea,
And we'll get our comfies on,
And chill and watch TV,
X factor or Strictly,
Just you and me,
And we'll both be knackered,
When we climb the stairs,
And we'll giggle at ourselves,
In our underwear,
And we'll hold hands while we're saying our prayers,
And we'll sleep and dream,
Like we have no cares.
Come on,
The sun's coming up,
What do you say?
Please wake up me love,
And be with me,
Just for one more day.

Pity the Lune

Rain falls pure from the heavens
On the fell where Ravens hail,
And gathers as the River Lune
 In Ravenstonedale,
Then laughs and trills in falls and rills,
And innocently glides
Towards the foot of Borrowdale,
Where Romans killed or compromised,
Then youthful and exuberant,
Gorging mountains, downward flows,
Where trains dash and cars crash,
And every day bloody the roads,
But pretty lies the prospect
Of Green Lonsdale past the kirk,
And underneath the bridge that lies,
Where Christians did the devil's work.
Then hesitant and faltering,
Unsure of what's to come,
Twists and turns to plot a course back home,
But, drawn away inexorably,
Westward to the sea,
Where crooked destiny now leads,
And creeps inevitably
Into the town where black clouds hung,
And righteous hymns to Him were sung,
Whilst all the time his traps were sprung,
On Gallows Hill where witches swung,

A town where beggars still doss down,
In the dark,
In the municipal park,
Deserted and doomed,
Past the quayside where slaves festooned
With chains, in pain, stood,
Marooned, in their new home,
Never to return to Sierra Leone!
Lost and alone!
Leave them all alone!
And rush down to the strand,
To the wet sand,
Where plovers land,
And flee!
Far out into the Irish Sea!
And bathe in equanimity,
And drown,
Far, far away, from people!
And from towns!

Rat

She had a rat in her attic,
This old lady with lilac hair,
It'd started to make her erratic,
So she stayed downstairs, she was scared.

This thing had happened dramatic,
One minute, it hadn't been there,
One minute she's enjoying a latte,
Next minute it's everywhere.

A rat with lamentable habits,
Eats everything, shits everywhere,
And peers down from up in the attic,
But when she looks up, it's not there.

There's a dirty brown rat in the attic,
That's scratching the floors and the shelves,
And performing peculiar antics,
And exuding a rat-nasty smell.

She always used to be happy,
Little girl with never a care,
She'd always been called charismatic
And cheered people up everywhere.

But her husband had been a fanatic,
In his manner, his clothes and his hair,
He made sure she was always kept at it,
He limited what she could wear.

She never quite knew how it happened,
Her mind must've been elsewhere,
They said that there'd been a bad accident
And her husband was no longer there.

And now she's a rat in her attic,
She can no longer go up the stairs,
She spends every day in a panic,
Sat by herself in her chair.

She's now got a rat in her attic,
So she has to take pills and say prayers,
She's got a big rat in her attic
And nobody cares!

Scarecrow

Jesus is hanging there,
He's stone dead.
He's like a scarecrow,
With a crown on his head,
And he died in vain,
He was misled,
He thought people listened
To the words he said,

Blessed are the landowners,
For they shall own the earth,

Blessed are the merchants,
Who'll get their money's worth,

Blessed are the imperialists,
Who plunder peoples lands,

Blessed are the witch burners,
For they shall warm their hands,

Blessed are the slavers,
For they shall all walk free,

Blessed are the governments,
Who keep us on our knees,

Blessed are the evangelists,
For they've no need to listen,

Blessed are the wealthy,
Whose gold and silver glistens,

And he thought the people listened,
Really listened to his words,
But his Beatitudes were wasted,
For this was all they'd heard,
And they raised him as an icon,
And nailed him to a tree,
Where he's just another scarecrow,
For nobody to see!

Some Boy's Grave

A blackbird lands, his eyes black suns,
Two swans at home where the pylons hum,
The track's all mud where the water comes,
When the tide gets high, where the river runs.
There are no crows here but a scarecrow stands,
And points both ways with the palms of his hands
To Sunderland Point, between sea and sand
Between heaven and earth where plovers land,

And, I don't think you should stand here today,
You'd better go back, go back the way you came,
Go back before you drown in the sea's impartial waves,
 In a Lune-grey grave, with a forgotten black slave.

This is the place where fortunes were made,
 By the white man's trade, that his god forgave,
He forgot that his son was sent here to save
The very souls he sent into slavery,
In those dark days, all our yesterdays
And tomorrows are the same, nothing's changed,
We're all deranged and stand here estranged,
Exposed as we gaze into destiny's black face.

And I don't think you should stand here today,
You'd better go back, go back the way you came,
Go back before you drown in the sea's impartial waves,
In a Lune-grey grave with a forgotten black slave.

In consecrated ground? An unmarked mound?
Stop and look around! Please, look all around!
Where hypocrisy abounds, and where deluded clowns,

Who consecrate our earth are blind and bound
In chains, their minds can't see our sanctity,
Regardless of our creeds, our colours, our abilities,
And this god of theirs demands only servility,
And his piety's profanity and idolatry, it's insanity.

And I don't think you should stand here today,
Go back, go back, go back the way you came,
Go back before you drown in the sea's impartial waves
In a Lune-grey grave with a forgotten black slave.

It's a cover up! In desolation!
Here lies hidden the shame of our whole nation,
One poor little soul who wasn't worth saving,
Shoved down a rabbit hole, forever degrading,
While the holy depraved, pretending they're praying,
Are enslaving us all by everything they're saying,
And it says everything in their guilty engraving,
It's not forgiveness their giving,
It's power they're craving!

But I think we should
All stand here today!
Because the tide has to turn
And wash all this away,
And we should stand here until
We're washed clean as slate,
Because it isn't too late
To change our ways,

I think we should all stand here today
In this forgotten place,

And accept the sea's embrace,
For the rest of our days,
Tended only by waves,
In this lonely enclave,
Some boy's grave.

That Day at the Allotment

We were down the allotment all morning,
And all that that entailed,
The sun shone gloriously,
Fun prevailed.
I'd had rabbits,
They'd had my turnip leaves.
Donal reckoned they were terrorists,
And said the jackdaws had something up their sleeves.
He was lucky,
They'd not touched his plot,
But I knew they were watching us,
From the perimeter,
The chattering hedgerow dwellers.
In the evening,
I went down again to water,
Some bloke stopped me at the gate,
Said "there'd been some drama down there,"
And I might want to keep away,
I went.
Donal had died there in the afternoon,
A heart attack while strimming.

"Lucky" I'd called him.
The undertakers were struggling
With his heavy body in a white sheet,
He was a dead weight.
And all the jackdaws,
And all the rabbits,
Were silent,
Silent now,
Watching from the perimeter hedgerows,
Something serious had happened.
And then they resumed their chatter,
And Donal was gone,
Ingloriously,
In the back of a black Volvo.

Bryan Griffin: Dances on the Lightside
Whimsy/Light Humour

The Long Lost summer

Oh, those almost forgotten summer days
Such long slow easy languorous ways.
Sultry heat heavily drifting on a breeze
As happy youth lingered in drowsy ease
Caressed by a hot suns kissing tease.

Oh, those almost forgotten summer days
Of verdant green in shimmering haze.
Azure seas stretching beyond horizons reach,
As youth frolicked on a hot sandy beach
We thought that life had nothing more to teach.
For the sparkling wine of our effervescent youth
Tasted of the heady promise of hope and truth.

Oh, those almost forgotten summer days
Distant memories found as we inward gaze.
For now we search for youths glowing ember
To warm the colder time of our September,
Our aged bones can rest whilst we remember.

Oh, those almost forgotten summer days
Time worn creases may form a winsome smile
As we again in merry youth linger for awhile
In the lost horizon of so many yesterdays,
Those almost mythical naive endless days.

Oh, those almost forgotten summer days,
Oh, those almost forgotten summer days.

I danced with my father

Sometimes in slumber memories of father form in clarity
and to the almost forgotten tempo of his life he dances
again with me.
In my childhood it was easy to keep step to his time for he
was my mentor in thought and deed divine.

Then came the angst and rebellion against his version of
truth, the dance became an angry Pasodoble of age versus
youth.
Manhood was a tango he still strove to command, but my
music was then played by a different band.

Come winter, those later years sliding into aged decline,
when his steps faltered as he danced out of time.
So, I took over the lead and for a while our dance was fine
but my days seemed short and we only danced when I
found the time.

And then the cruel finality as I held on tightly to his hand
while my father hesitantly danced into another land.
Now the dance is mine as I waltz each hour away, my heart
still yearns for my father's knowing steps throughout my
yesterday.

In the fifties when I was born

In the nineteen fifties if I recall the time right, life, like a
Bush television was viewed in black and white.
Outgrown clothes passed from child to child was the norm,
in that distant decade in which I was born.
The clacking Singer sewing machine was a familiar sight as
Mother let out clothes that became too tight.
During Christmas we waited patiently for the Queen, who,
would talk to us through a twelve-inch screen.

Politicians all dressed the same in unison they'd say
"austerity "was the watchword of the day.
A time of recovery from the devastations of war when
mothers accepted the words of Dr Seuss as law.
On Sundays off to church to show that we conform, in the
afternoon dads would mow the lawn.
On scratched vinyl records Lonnie Donegan sang "Sweet
Sixteen". In cinemas we saw a moody James Dean.

The fifties a dull time of thick navy serge and a correctness
that the sixties would come to purge.
Our cities seemed fogged in cold swirling grey where
working class people laboured long for little pay.
A place of bombed out streets and buildings by the score, a
vista of rubble scattered the landscapes floor.
A country rebuilt by proud survivors of Hitler's scourge, an
Era when homosexuals must hide natures urge.

Thus, my childhood was spent in a landscape of grey a
bastion of strict morals for living the right way.
A pause in time to help in the world's reconstruction, a
needed recovery from the previous decade's destruction.
As my teens beckoned a new decade was on its way the
promise of colourful times heady and gay.
A future time, when youth unbounded needed no
instruction, would be full of promise, naïvetés and a pinch
of corruption.

A Benchmark

This is where weary travellers rest their tired feet,
The place aged matrons' gossip, illicit lovers meet.
A bed for the inebriated to sleep away all their woe,
The static point that marks life's frenetic to and fro.

It was a kind donation from someone long ago dead.
A tranquil place from where the birds are easily fed.
The Aves reciprocate appreciation in splats of stench,
Mottling the weathered green paint of the park bench.

The Park

Bordered by a towns red brick history
Encapsulating natures manifold mystery,
Lies a wonderful tree lined grassy space
Where people escape from life's fast pace
To witness the seasons changing scene
From golden brown to verdant green.
By a lake where swans glide with ease.
A Brass band echoes tradition in the breeze.

On aged park benches occupants contemplate
For the past and present seems to resonate
In a dogs bounding joy or a child's happy cry
Catching the wind to mask a lover's whispered sigh,
As people ambling tread the paths of the past
In and out of dancing shadows by tall trees cast.

Here in towering trees the birds chorus sing
Of lazy summer Sundays as the church bells ring.
Whilst tennis balls whizz to and fro in frenetic attack
And bowls are rolled aimed to gently kiss the jack.

Oh lucky the town, though times be grim and stark,
That despite its travails boasts a glorious public park.

January Rain

It's a rain misted, dark clouded, wet grey day
When cold damp airs bite holds all in its sway.
With each tree and flower drooping in disarray
As from bowed leaf to leaf water slowly drips away,
To fall to the soaked earth where puddles abound
Mirroring cloud grey reflections upon the ground.

Awakened frogs sing a short lamenting sound.
Surfacing worms wriggle up to make a muddy mound
And fishes rise from the deep dark depths to eat
As raindrops hit the surface water to a drip drop beat.
Swirling eddies of racing water seem to compete
Gushing helter-skelter through the gutters of the street.

As soulfully through steamed windows we gaze
Not seeing the beauteous wonder of nature's ways,
Remembering the sunshine of much warmer days
We forget even grey clouded nature deserves our praise.

Arcadia

Where is Arcadia, not lost, perhaps found in our sleep,
where piping Shepherds watch the flocks in their keep.

The sheep graze on verdant grass which is lush and deep,
whilst we, in this bewitching idyll, sweet accord doth reap.

Morecambe Bay

Resplendent in its flat golden desolation, the beach
Stretches out to be lost in the faraway of horizons reach.
Here quicksand travels beneath the surface as if to defy
In its shifting, a quiet treachery to even the wariest eye.

Swooping, swirling above in the slow dying of the light
Gulls harshly shriek their anger at the oncoming night.
Shallows, trapped pools left behind by the seas retreat
Twinkle starlight making the sense of isolation complete.

The Bluebell

I went to a place where bluebells used to grow, there I
found discarded empty warehouses all in a row.
From a crack in the concrete a single bluebell grew,
stretching upwards to the sky reflecting its hue.

I was tempted to take it home to give it loving care, but
then I realised it was far better growing there
As it danced gracefully to the gentle song of the wind, my
spirit was somehow lifted and cheerfully I grinned.

The Swans

As light was receding giving way to dusk, I saw them gliding
regally across the water beautiful and fey.
Spectral they seemed as with ghost like grace the pair
effortlessly travelled on their watery way.

The river murmured a love sonnet in tribute to their poise
as upon its surface stars danced a jig of delight.
I felt that any moment perhaps the gentle ringing laughter
of fairies might herald the coming night.

Maybe I heard them in a dream or surrendered to some
sweet enchantment to hear the ancients sing.
Pan's persuasive pipes in dulcet tones with Diana's laughter
like soft tinkling chimes accompanying.

Regardless, my soul was filled as the Swans passed by on
their eternal journey down the rivers winding way.
As I watched in total awe, I knew that no art of man could
match in grace or to their beauty homage pay.

Finally gone, the dusk surrendered to night, the waters
lapped sing song as by the breeze it was caressed.
Reluctantly as I travelled homeward a certainty grew that
by some ancient divination I had been possessed.

A flight of fancy

The air was still and sultry, filled with honeysuckle scent,
evening shade was hovering, the day was nearly spent.
I strolled lazily about my garden appreciating the floral fare,
blithely enjoying my cigar, relaxed without a care.

Was it a mirage, a trick of shadowing light? For something
caught my eye perhaps a dragonfly in flight.
Amidst the abundance of apple blossom something moved
with a furtiveness that any cat would have approved.

I neared the apple tree inquisitive as to what I might see. I
peered into the blossoms, quick as a flash, it broke free.
I was startled as it sped before my eyes with such alacrity,
though still sceptical I must admit it could have been a fairy.

Radiance

Light,
Illuminating the vast heavens at night countless stars twinkling blue bright sending lustrous messages from the past arriving on earth from a universe vast.

Light,
The Sun shines upon his Sister Moon, who reflects her luminescent boon to dance and sparkle upon waters of the night, whilst wolves sing homage to Luna bright.

Light,
Emerging from the blush red dawn, a glowing herald of a new day doth form illuminating bedroom window frames, gently kissing away the nights remains.

Light,
Verdant greenery reaches out to the sun to feed upon the energy of a new day begun. Whilst a rainbow, a spectrum of sunlight forms a bridge of wondrous delight.

Light,
Unbowed by time or the universes endless night, travelling giver of life, thou wonder, **thou light**

Polka Dots

I sat outside sipping summer from rich Chianti wine, the sun upon my skin, tingling warmth, a caressing tease.
With lazy ease I gazed down the street to see a vision divine, her polka dot dress lazily fluttering in a gentle breeze.

Like a swan's watery glide, she sailed into view a lithe tanned body wrapped in polka dot blue and white.
Shiny black hair danced in tune with a long-legged stride, amused green eyes met mine, a captivating sight.

I wanted to passionately claim her heart, could a shy, plain dullard possess something so perfect.
Transfixed, glass in trembling hand, watching her slowly depart, I continued drinking, forlornly abject.

The Far Country

There are no boundaries embraced within your arms. No rules exist as I tenderly explore your many charms.

Death holds no dominion as we unite in the dance of life. Entwined we banish thoughts of fear and strife,

We ride the stormy seas of desire, wild and free, until, our passions spent, we lie stilled in quiet harmony.

The world is our bed as we in calmed serenity lie curled in each other's arms dreaming of a brave new world.

Blue eyes

They can be ice cold a steel grey reprimand
Or hold secrets I may never understand.
Oh those dammed eyes of clear Azure blue,
A steady gaze that I simply drown into.

They draw me in with mischievous delight
Or be the soulfully sad aftermath of a fight.
Oh those dammed eyes of clear Azure blue,
No hidden subterfuge, just steady and true.

They can adore, making me feel like a King
Or transfix me to set my heart abeating
They can turn me into a tongue tied fool
Or can be as still and calm as a placid pool
Oh those damned eyes of clear Azure blue,
A constant beacon lighting me home to you.

Aphrodite

Porcelain skinned,
Classic perfection,
Hides a soul
Blind to love.

Love for Sale

Colette had slowly turned from me
To stare from her window balcony.
She made such a beauteous sight
Wrapped in a halo of morning light.
For her mind was now elsewhere
It was as if I was no longer there
And to this alluring courtesan
I had become just another man.

Her lips, her body, I could possess
She gave me passion as my mistress,
But her thoughts were hers alone
her silent moments I could not own.
In that moment I could see a sad irony
For it was she who owned my soul completely
It was I who was enslaved by her you see.

Auburn

Auburn hair drifting lightly in the breeze, ringlets sprouting
a haphazard tease, adorning a face kissed gently by the sun,
a freckled button nose wrinkled in fun.

Full red lips pout, a wry smile begins to form, amused clear
blue sparkling eyes adorn the calm beauty of a classically
elegant face. A long slender neck adding to form and grace.

Small pert breasts enhance a tomboy frame, long willowy
legs a promise of joy to gain. A living example of womanly
perfection, To ensure the male libido an erection.

A problem that my adoring eyes did discern the Adams apple caused hesitant concern. Some happily orbit such worlds with no bother reared by a much less disapproving mother.

Unfortunately, as liberal as I try hard to be an Adams apple is just a bite too far for me.

Just a helpful Hand

It arrived in the post a box addressed to me.
I opened it ripping the fancy wrapping free.
It was clean, well-manicured, nothing grand
After all it seemed just like any other hand.
The fact it was disembodied was of concern,
Its evil intent, the terror of it, I was soon to learn.

Moving with swift agility it was malevolently bold
It launched itself at my throat and grabbed hold.
Its strong fingers tightened trying to strangle me,
I struggled but managed to break the grip free.

Thrust back in the box and parcelled as before,
I placed it in the post addressed to my *mother-in-law*.

Dancing in the Moonlight

The ladies Camberwell black magic coven regularly meets every Thursday.
They discard their corsets to worship Beelzebub in a middle-class way.
After a glass or two of sherry they ceremonially don a mask to cover their face.
With feverish naked abandon they dance swaying to the music of Liberace.
What a chilling scene to behold, matronly ladies cavorting devil may care,
false teeth gnash as ecstatic groans and moans add horror to the affair.
Finally, as Midnight chimes, they offer their knitting to Menzies the goat.
At Friday's Women's Institute meeting they wink at each other and gloat.
After deciding charitable deeds to support they discuss the book of the day.
Whilst all the time a tingle with girlish glee looking forward to their next Soiree.

Sign Language

I use two fingers to gesture defy and use one to gesture goodbye.

A simple thread of thought

What does the spider do during those long waits?
Perhaps in the pensive stillness he meditates,
Contemplating upon life's meaning as he rests,
Awaiting the winged bugs or leggy insect pests.

Whilst he sucks out his snared victims juices
Perhaps he justifies his actions with excuses.
Maybe blaming it upon one of nature's jests
That amidst the webs silken beauty he ingests.

Consider how, in his long sojourn, he spends time
Awaiting the silken thread to signal when to dine.
If not spent in a deep thoughtful contemplation
How tediously boring must be a spider's vocation.

Loophole

In the American constitution
The founding fathers resolution
Gives gun user's absolution.

Then the answer is logically
If a gun ban cannot be made legally
To ban all the bullets, you see.

Infamy

Once I was top dog Rome's No 1 Geezer
I was Julie C the guy they called Caesar
I was Numero Uno, a love god, Rome's stud
Yes even sex pot Cleo said I was reeeal good

Sadly-*Infamy, Infamy they all had it in-fer- me*

Then I was the big generalissimo -I never lost a war
I said Veni Vedi Vici and wowed the senate floor
But now comes the woeful part of my life's history
Beware the ides of March, I thought mere sophistry

Oh No--*Infamy, Infamy they all had it in-fer- me* '

That bugger Brutus and pals green with jealousy
Decided to stab me in the back you see
They planned and plotted until came the day
To stabbed me in the back as I said Et tu, Brute?"

Thrice Woe--*Infamy, Infamy they all had it in-fer- me*

So, open yer lug holes and take advice from Julie C
If you wish to avoid a Shakespearean tragedy
Never turn your back on your enemy or friend,
Particularly in March to evade the sharp end

cus -*Infamy, Infamy they all had it in-fer- me*

Getting Wet

Life will swamp you, stay afloat, persevere become a boat.
Be willing to drift into each day, let the current lead your
way.
Until you find your course, do not drown in a sea of
remorse. There will be rapids ahead, to survive just keep a
clear head.
As you journey the river of life, a winding way of joy and
strife, you must hold to what is true, the rudder and
compass are you.
Though rough waters deny your will you'll remain steady,
not spill. The journey will be a life's labour ending in home
the safe harbour.

Unity

What is the meaning of unity?
Maybe, a concord with the world community?
Standing together so that we can succeed
In places where ignorance and bigotry breed.
Or perhaps to recognise accord in the diversity
Of all the cultures that enrich humanity.
For the sky is blue the earth is green
And we should find harmony in all between.
As different streams find their way to the sea
So it is with all differences in theology,
There should be no reason for singular entitlement,
All faiths seek the same road to enlightenment.
I believe this small but powerful word unity
Defines that in divergence there can be parity.

Rowland Crowland : Dances on the Lightside
Whimsy/Light Humour

Heaven (1977)

Pretty, downtrodden, Jewish mums,
On their way to heaven,
Poorly shod and
Pushing prams,
Round Salford 7.
I saw you just a moment ago,
Down the bottom of Leicester Road,
It made me feel sad, when I saw you,
I hoped you were trudging home,
But now you're at the top here,
On the on the road near Heaton Park
And I bet you'll feel so weary
By the time that it gets dark!
I'd like to buy you a coffee,
Or a cup of tea and a cake,
A cream horn or a piece of banoffee
We could have it, by the lake!
I'd get you something colourful to wear,
And I'd laugh and hold your hand,
I'd love to wash and blow your hair,
And spray you all over with Paco Rabanne!
I'd take off your shoes and we'd dance in the park,
And lie on the grass in the sun,
And fall asleep till nearly dark,
Then saunter home,
Smiling and tired and satisfied,

With some memories to share,
Feeling good and warm inside,
Not bothered that people would stare,
Because I'm a bum and having fun
Is my idea of heaven,
While you're destined to push your pram,
Round Salford 7.

In Trees.

In trees,
You'll notice the breeze
Lingers.
It brings you things from far away,
Like how the sea's doing,
What the weather will be like today,
And whether to expect the rain.
In trees,
There's a sense of
Quiet living things
That's pleasing,
Lineages of insects , birds, invertebrates
Getting on with things,
At their ease.
In trees,
There's stillness and movement.
In trees,
There's life, death and rebirth,
From roots to leaves,

In seeds,
There's almost timelessness.
In trees
There's togetherness,
And solitude,
And almost silence,
And cacophonous noise
When the wind blows
And each leaf shouts with its own voice.
In trees,
All along,
There's been bird song,
And the birds will tell you
What's going on,
And what is right,
And what is wrong,
If you listen to them,
In trees.

Manic Depression.

Manic depression, has
Captured my soul, it can
Flaming well keep it!

Butterfly

A goblin friend once said to me,
As we sat by the bank of a stream,
"Zhuangzi sat in this self – same spot,
When he dreamed his butterfly dream.
Yes, Zhuangzi sat in this self-same spot,
When he dreamed his butterfly dream."
So we closed our eyes,
And spread our wings,
Flew up in smoke,
To the Realm of Kings,
As ravens on a sudden breeze,
Like turtles through the summer seas,
We swam,
We ran,
We burrowed deep,
Then stopped in time,
In endless sleep,
A million years
Rained through our tears
And all our worries,
All our fears,
Gone and done,
We fell to earth,
And into birth by the banks of a stream,
Where a butterfly once fell from a dream.

The goblin gave his lute a twang
And winked at me before he sang,
"Never let Confucian rules
Add to your confusion,
Illusion's just reality,
Reality's just illusion."

Sonnet Written in a Chippy

Deep in your pockets there's coins jingling
There's ready ships rustling and vinegar chinking
 There's pies on a hot plate, puddings in a steamer,
This is a place to sit and dream,
On the wooden bench that runs under the window
And outside it's cold, and forever the wind blows
It's dark and it's raining, the windows steamed up
And time stands still for some chips and a pie
And just for a moment you're warm inside
And safe and sound and the people in the queue
Are chatting and laughing, they're feeling it too!
Then it's…. "Hey you over there composing a sonnet
Wake up cock do you want gravy on it?!!"

Forgiveness

Evening stillness,
Ducks' wings whistle,
A heron fishes,
Birch leaves glisten,
Scintillating,
The wind whispers,
Sibilant,
Like vespers
Forgive us our trespasses
And forgive those
Who trespass against us,
Forgive everything
And
   Just
      Listen.

Oystercatchers.

Oystercatchers,
Hard by the Bay,
Steadfast,
Braced against the rain.
Legs rigid,
Wings folded,
Fixed into the wind,
Bold, sea-cold,
Birds of the coastal plain.
I first saw them off Fegla Fawr,
Big red beaks like I'd never seen before,
I sat and watched them from afar,
Oystercatchers, Wow!
And now they're here on Morecambe Bay,
Unmistakeable, standing that way,
A panoply of piebald,
All facing Ireland
Through the sea spray.
Look!
For flying in a straight line
There's got to be no match,
There's no time to deviate,
When there's oysters to catch!
I can see them from Marine Road,
It's the place where oystercatchers go,
For cockles and mussels by the tractor load,
I've never seen one catch an oyster though!
But there they go,
Stepping staccato,

Red stiletto
Legs with backward knees,
Rooting, tooting,
Shooting the breeze,
Pied pipers,
Whistling like referees!
Red-eyed, intent
On serious deeds.
You can keep your peregrines,
You can keep your golden eagles,
Here's majesty enough for me
Standing proud amongst the seagulls.
And then, as one, they're gone!
And I'm off to buy a mug,
With an oystercatcher on!

Another Autumn Poem

The meadow sweet has seen its best,
The people on the street are restless,
Birch leaves whisper their distress,
The river's choked, the leaves are a mess.

The wind just came and changed everything
Without invitation, it blew a new year in,
That's cold and dark and turning into
"Long time till the spring."

The crows are croaking, "What's going on?"
The geese have sensed it, they've gone,
And left a feeling of being alone,
Like somehow lost, like "away from home,"

Like where have all the hours gone?
It's no wonder the birds have flown
To winter lands where they look on,
As only bonfires warm our bones.

And night it turns to water-colour day,
Then black-ink night again and stays,
A glimmer at the end of days
Is all that's left to light our ways,

But shimmering gold there in the lake,
Awakens, and the breaths you take
Are crystal clear and deeply slaking
Like there's birth in this strange state

Of death that's all around descended,
Why would life and death be blended
Somewhere where the light has ended?
It's like death has just pretended

There's no chance for anyone,
And told us that the world is done,
But in that moment we've begun
To dance forever round the Sun!

Besom

It's time to dance to ancient tunes,
And heed the weaving of the loom,
The inner heaving of the moon,
The sweeping of the besom broom,
Pretty, whippy, birch tree tips,
So many secrets on the lips,
Where magik drips like amber mead,
Upon your steeds who take the sky,
Nine words to keep, nine worlds to fly,
See the besoms sweeping by,
Hold on fast, the ash shaft,
And let go as you ride!
Legs astride, thrilling inside,
And rising in spirals,
In trance and inspired,
Inhibition swept aside,
You glide like fat geese,
And arrive, released,
From worldly matricide.

Keer Cormorants

I sailed slowly down the Keer,
Where Cormorants hang
Around the estuary,
They're kind of like a gang.
There is a queer feeling here,
Eels meet here,
And head for the Kent,
Intent on breeding,
Like all life's believing
What's meant to be
Is unequivocally
Just meant,
No argument,
And all time,
Is time well spent.

Temple

And Jesus did rush into the temple,
And did cause a great deal of alarm,
The doors flung open wide,
A cold pharisee cried,
"What's the matter with you?
Where you born in a barn!!!?"

Murmuration

Crows,
A great cloud of
Them, and jackdaws like smoke,
Over the woods rising, their noise a cacophony

They're mesmerising, organised
Chaos, their voices,
Orchestrated,
Raucous,
Yet venerated, forever
Grating, then still, oak leaves
Rustle, like applause,
Crows and jackdaws,
Now they're
Roosting
Till
Dawn.

Heart Sutra

All form is emptiness,
And emptiness is form,
And nothing ever, ever dies,
And nothing's ever born.

Autumn Dawn

Blood red haws in the dawning sun,
A piebald horse gallops for fun,
A wonderful morning has begun,
The crows and jackdaws have come home,
The gorse amber now, almost dun,
A westerly wind blows the tide upon
The salt flats that I'm standing on
And in the distance a hunter's gun
Echoes off the crag at Warton
And geese trace the estuary where the Keer runs
Into the bay, and then gone,
Today, flown away, beyond
The understanding of anyone.
Why did the horse run?
Where have the geese gone?
Why do the crows come home?
Why is it wonderful?
What will the gorse become?
What of the hunter's gun?
Why did the day dawn?
And wherefore the sun?
Why did the wind blow?
Where does the tide go?
How can we ever know
Why things are done?
But one thing I do know, it's there in the haws glow,
All things are one! Yes, all things are one!

At the Doctors

A goblin face on each of my fingertips,
Ten little goblins in a row,
And the condition has started on my toes now
But the Doctor knows.
I'm sitting in his surgery right now,
I think he's thinking "cream,"
Beause he's flicking methodically through his BNF,
But he seems in a bit of a dream.
He looks tired, pressured, exasperated,
Doctors suffer like this,
One second he seems angry, then distracted,
It's stress that's what it is! It's stress!
When I called because I'd swallowed a tree spirit,
I remember he'd looked just fine,
Stress comes and goes in professionals,
He's probably not like this all the time.
But his job must be horrendous,
And he's probably got a wife and kids,
And a big expensive car to run,
 And hugely inflated household bills.
Now he's frantically flicking the pages,
He's desperate to find the right cream,
 He looks like he could flip into a rage,
 This is what dedication means!
Now, is there a way I can help him?
Because I just hate to see him upset,
So I wiggle all ten fingers at him and say,
"Doctor, have you found our goblin finger cream yet?"

Vampire

I saw this bloke on Tib Street,
Dressed like a vampire,
He was swift on his feet,
He was on a flier.
Next minute he's in the shop,
Buying dried apricots,
The place went still,
He left everyone in shock,
Jackie said, "He's a vampire,
Yeh, he's a real vampire,
He drinks blood,"
I suppose he would!
You don't see him in the daytime,
Unless he comes in the shop,
But he never stops.
He wears a black suit,
His face is white as ash,
He hangs around the backs,
Where we put out the trash.
Jackie said, "He wears a sash,"
It's probably from Affleck's Palace
It's blood red, he's pure dread,
Jackie said, "He's supposed to be dead,
But he's one of the undead,
He uses a coffin for a bed."
To me, he's just plastered his face with cheese spread
Because he's not too right in the head!

Virus. (1977)

It's the virus!
It's back!
I thought it was going to get me the sack!
I just let the foreman scream and shout!
I said "it's just one of those bugs,
That's been going about."
He reckoned I was swinging the lead.
"I don't even know what that means," I said,
He ranted and raved, but when he let me speak,
I told him Ivy Rowbottom had had it last week,
And I hadn't seen her swinging any lead!
"Just get back to your job!" he said,
"And do some work, you're doing my head in!"
It's a mad job anyway and the money's a pittance,
So I don't really know why it is that I stay,
It's just really so I can pave my own way,
But I can't see me turning in come what may,
For the rest of mi life, driving mi crazy,
Making kilowatt bulbs every blinding day!
I'm just waiting for something
To light my way!
To something new,
That I can do,
That I'd like to do, day after day!
And I'd be healthy and happy that day!
And I'd enjoy just making my way,
And I'd enjoy just earning my pay!
And I'd enjoy just being me,
And going out after breakfast,

And coming home for my tea,
And spending the evening with my family,
Then settle for the night all tucked up,
And when I draw the curtains,
I'll look forward to work,
Then you wouldn't find me shirking,
With a virus!

Solstice

Hunkered down in a winter storm,
In a bunker to us safe from harm,
We've oak and ash logs in our arms,
We need a fire to keep us warm,
I strike a spark form flint and steel,
With kindling in my hands I'm kneeling,
I'm going to tell you how I feel,
And then I'll cook us one last meal,
I'm scared and hungry I'm tired and cold,
I don't know when I got so old,
Unless there's fire I'll never hold
You close, our stories won't unfold,
But this small spark won't ignite the tinder,
And look right there outside the window,
It's bleak and black and the great north wind blows,
It's surely death it's going to bring us,
Our lives are spent in cheating and lying,
There's no one left who isn't crying
Inside themselves whilst endlessly trying

To live a life that's not spent dying,
And all along you've seen me here,
I'm cold and dark and I'm disappearing,
There's never any warmth in this dreary
Life that's so very nearly leaving,
But wait, little flames are burning bright,
Something's happening here tonight,
And in our hearth something just might
Melt the ice that holds us tight,
It's in the very firelight,
This tiny flame that's been ignited,
Within the black and endless night,
Its sparks have set the stars alight!
Life is here and is for living,
Things are ending yet beginning,
And at the very point of leaving,
Is the light you must believe in,
Something deep inside is stirring,
Something sprung from endless yearning,
It's just the firelight that's burning,
But something magical's returning,
      Solstice!
        Solstice!
          Solstice!

My God Eileen

Why would you have a god called god?
I just think it's really very odd!
It's like having a dog called dog,
Or a job called job,,
Or a wife called wife
Or a cat called cat,
And just how stupid's that?!
And why does he have to be a man?
Is that some kind of master plan?
Like a woman can't give birth to mankind,
But a man can!
What sort of mad scam's that, man?
No, if I had a god,
She'd have a name,
Like Eileen,
Or Veronica,
Or maybe Jane,
And I'd walk with her,
Holding hands,,
And I'd talk with her
We'd walk along the sand
At the edge of the sea,
And I'd lie in her arms,
And dream,
While Autumn leaves fell on me,
And I'd love her,
And I'd make love to her,

And always be her devotee.
Yes, my god would be a she-god,
She'd smell of incense,
And make more sense
Than a he-god,
Thinking he's holier than me,
Thinking he can control me,
Thinking he's got some weird ungodly hold over me,
Who knows if I don't go to church on Sunday,
And who'll scold me!
No, mine's a female god
Who'll hold me,
She'll enfold me in her arms,
And keep me safe from harm,
And console me,
And say I'm as good as everyone else,
And that I'm worth something as well,
As just walking around down here,
In fear!
She'll be someone who'll hear me when I'm crying,
Someone who won't judge me when I'm lying,
Someone who'll comfort me when I'm dying,
Someone sublime,
Someone serene,
My god,
Eileen!

Epilogue

Dear readers, we do hope you enjoyed our dance with words and that it may inspire those inclined to also put pen to paper.

"Let the beauty of what you love be what you do"

Rumi
(1273 to 1273)